*intro*

"Why are you writing a devotional for ladies? You're men."

Guilty as charged. We're men. But we have a vested interest in the spiritual lives of women. First, we're directly attached to a number of women: we both have mothers who are women, we both have wives who are women, and between us we have six daughters (and no sons).

More seriously, we're both privileged to pastor women. We labor together at Tri-County Bible Church in Madison, Ohio. It's a robust body of believers, roughly half of whom are ladies. These devotionals were originally written for them, the women under our pastoral care.

Finally, we're writing because of the relative scarcity of sound materials available for Christian women. There are happy exceptions, for which we're grateful, but much of what is commonly written for ladies lacks biblical depth and doctrinal accuracy. That's a problem—women need solid Gospel meat as surely as their male counterparts.

We hope you will use this resource to enhance your study of the Scriptures, not to replace it. Whether you're studying on your own or with other ladies, we urge you to read the biblical passage suggested for each day in addition to our effort to unpack it. The articles are arranged fairly randomly. Some describe what it means to be a Christian. Others address singleness, marriage, or motherhood. Most address an aspect of Christian growth. But all highlight the way the Gospel of Jesus Christ affects everyday life. That's the passion of our lives and of the church we pastor. We're all about the Gospel—meditating on it in our worship, encouraging each other with it, and sharing it with the lost.

We affectionately dedicate these studies to our lovely wives, Lori Anderson and Hannah Tyrpak, who are "far more precious to us than jewels" (Proverbs 31:10). They provide us with daily examples of what godly wives, mothers, and believers look like. We both "married up," and we continually praise the Lord for their ministries to and with us.

May the Lord use *Gospel Meditations for Women* to drive you Christ-ward, and may all glory go to Him (Psalm 115:1).

For the sake of His name,

Chris Anderson & Joe Tyrpak

Grace Abounding More than Sin
READ MATTHEW 1

And David was the father of Solomon by the wife of Uriah.
MATTHEW 1:6

The very first words of the New Testament are a record of Jesus Christ's ancestors. Though we're prone to skip over all the "begats" (to quote the KJV), they contain vital lessons regarding Jesus and His saving mission. The first chapter of Matthew records the genealogy of Jesus Christ, by which Matthew proves that Jesus was a descendant of both Abraham and David (1:1). As such, Jesus was able to fulfill God's covenant promises to both men—He was the long-awaited descendant of Abraham in whom all the nations of the earth would be blessed (Genesis 22:18), and He was the long-awaited descendant of David whose throne would be established forever (2 Samuel 7:12-13).

While the genealogy mentions 42 men, it also mentions five women: Tamar (1:3), Rahab (1:5), Ruth (1:5), "the wife of Uriah" (1:6), and Mary (1:16). Other than Mary, each of these women had some black stain on their reputation. Let's review some biblical details regarding each of them.

Tamar is the young widow who disguised herself as a cult prostitute on the roadside in order to seduce Judah, her lustful father-in-law, into an incestuous relationship. The distressing story is told in Genesis 38. Even though Judah came to admit his wrong, saying, "She is more righteous than I" (38:26), there is no question that both were blatantly unrighteous.

Rahab was a prostitute in the Canaanite city of Jericho. She was known not simply as "Rahab," but as "Rahab the prostitute" (Joshua 2 and 6). In other words, she had a well-known reputation as an immoral woman.

Ruth, like Rahab, was a Gentile. Worse than that, she was a Moabite. Moab was the son of Lot's incestuous daughter (Genesis 19:37) and the father of an idolatrous nation that would be known for centuries as Israel's enemy (Judges 3 and 11). Further, Ruth was so destitute that she was entirely dependent on other people's charity. Finally, she was the widow of a man whose Jewish family had gone to "sojourn in the country of Moab" (Ruth 1:1), a decision which evidenced little wisdom on the part of Ruth's in-laws.

Bathsheba, "the wife of Uriah," was infamous for her adultery with King David (2 Samuel 11-12). Although David bore the greater responsibility for the sin, Bathsheba openly bathed in view of the king's palace, slept with David, and went along with his cover-up strategy.

There you have it—Jesus' great-grandmothers included an incestuous daughter-in-law, a prostitute, a Moabite beggar, and an adulteress. (Do you feel like you need a bath?) What do we learn here? That Jesus doesn't mind associating with sinners, that Jesus saves sinners, and that Jesus graciously uses sinners to accomplish His good will.

The angel told Joseph to name Mary's child *Jesus* because He would be the one to save His people from their sins (1:21). Craig Blomberg connected Jesus' saving mission with His genealogy when he wrote, "If the Messiah can be born from this kind of ancestry, he can be a deliverer for all kinds of people, even disreputable ones" (*Jesus and the Gospels*, 199). God, in His grace, saves and uses people like us.

Let the Gospel alleviate your guilt for past sins. —JOE

The Righteous for the Unrighteous
READ ISAIAH 53

For Christ also suffered once for sins,
the righteous for the unrighteous, that he might bring us to God.
1 PETER 3:18

The greatest need of every person in the world—male or female, married or single, rich or poor—is to be reconciled to God. Our most urgent problem is not physical, financial, political, or social, but spiritual. Scripture repeatedly teaches that our sin separates us from God (Isaiah 59:2), resulting not only in our guilt before Him, but in a great spiritual chasm between us. We need God above all else, but our sin has estranged us from Him. What's to be done, then? How can the divide between the holy God and sinful men and women be bridged? Though religious opinions abound, Scripture provides the authoritative answer in 1 Peter 3:18.

The verse begins by teaching that "Christ suffered once for sins," an obvious allusion to Jesus' death on the cross. Though Christ's crucifixion seems to be a tragedy, it was actually His ultimate triumph and the only means by which He could rescue sinners. Shockingly, Jesus not only suffered at the hands of murderous men, but also at the hands of God, who punished the Lord Jesus for the sins of the world (Isaiah 53:6, 10). That's the point of the phrase "the righteous for the unrighteous." Christ died as a *substitute*. Jesus is "the righteous [one]." He has never sinned. He is described by God as "My beloved Son, with whom I am well pleased" (Matthew 3:17). Why, then, would the sinless one suffer for sins? Because He died for the sins of *others*—"the unrighteous," an unflattering but accurate description of sinners like us. Whereas we deserve to be forsaken and punished by God, now and for eternity, Jesus was forsaken and punished by God in our place (Matthew 27:46). The Father treated the Son as though He were a criminal, pouring out the very last drop of His wrath against sinners on the righteous as though He were the unrighteous. Jesus thus appeased (or propitiated) God by absorbing the punishment our sin deserved (Romans 3:24-25).

Christ's suffering on behalf of sinners was infinitely dreadful, but it is complete: He "suffered *once* for sins." Jesus' saving work cannot be repeated or amended. Though religions attempt to prolong the suffering required for forgiveness—saying that Jesus' sacrifice must be repeated through the Mass, or that sinners must suffer in Purgatory, or that we must earn our way to God by good works—the Bible insists that Jesus' death was sufficient to save sinners. "It is finished" was Christ's triumphant cry at His death (John 19:30)!

Why did Christ, the sinless Son of God, endure such agony? "That he might bring us to God." As discussed earlier, our greatest need is peace with God. Though we have a "God-shaped hole" in our hearts, we are estranged from Him by our unrighteousness. Jesus' death met our desperate need by providing a way for sinners to be brought to God. Because of Jesus, we can be reconciled instead of at war; welcomed instead of exiled; blessed instead of condemned. Jesus' is your bridge to God. You can know God and have peaceful, joyous fellowship with Him, all because of Christ. Will you turn from your sins and trust in Jesus?

Let the Gospel save your soul. —CHRIS

The Triumph of Christian Joy
READ PHILIPPIANS 4 & HABAKKUK 3:16-19

Rejoice in the Lord always; again I will say, Rejoice.

PHILIPPIANS 4:4

Were I asked to describe the typical person in Bible-believing churches, a lot of words would come readily to mind. Unfortunately, *joyful* would not be among them. We have tragically come to believe that one can be godly and yet morose and unpleasant, as though joy weren't listed among the fruits of a Spirit-controlled life (Galatians 5:22-23) and as though Christ's promises that we would experience *full* joy were empty (John 15:11; 16:24). The idea that gloominess (or grumpiness!) is next to godliness is disgusting. Martin Lloyd-Jones, perhaps the greatest English preacher of the 20ᵗʰ century, agrees. He addressed the problem throughout his classic book *Spiritual Depression.* Here's a taste:

> *"We must face this problem [of joyless Christians] for the sake of the Kingdom of God and for the glory of God. In a sense a depressed Christian is a contradiction in terms, and he is a very poor recommendation for the gospel" (foreword).*

Throughout the Scriptures we are commanded(!) to be joyful. Philippians 4:4 is one such passage. Paul, the imprisoned Apostle, wrote to the suffering, persecuted church at Philippi (where he had once been beaten, imprisoned and expelled [Acts 16]) and insisted that they "rejoice in the Lord always." How is that possible?

First, we must understand the meaning of joy. When Paul commands us to "rejoice," he's not calling for giddiness. Joy isn't a stupid grin or a Pollyanna attitude that denies hard circumstances. Indeed, there may be joy alongside tears rather than smiles. Why? Because joy is gladness and contentedness of soul, not merely a feeling of happiness.

Next, and most importantly, we must understand the source of joy. Scripture commands us to rejoice *in the Lord.* That's not just a pious way of saying, "Be happy in a Christian way." Rather, it's telling us the secret to joy: joy comes from our relationship with God, who Himself is omni-joyful! The key to moving from self-pity to genuine joy is not thinking happy thoughts; it's thinking of and fellowshipping with Christ!

Finally, we must understand the triumph of joy. Paul doesn't say that we are to rejoice only when the economy is good, when our children are behaving, when our house is squeaky clean, or when we're healthy. He commands us to rejoice *always,* like he did in prison (Philippians 1:4-7 and 2:17-18), like Habakkuk did in the midst of war and destruction (Habakkuk 3:17-19), and like believers have done in tragic circumstances throughout history.

Can we rejoice in the midst of tragedy? We can if our joy is rooted *in the Lord. Your joy will be as constant as its cause.* If you find your greatest pleasure and satisfaction in Jesus Christ, you can rejoice all the time. If you set your hopes elsewhere, you'll be another miserable believer—and the world has already seen enough of those contradictions.

Let the Gospel affect your outlook on life. —CHRIS

The Gospel Crushes Relational Conflict

READ 1 CORINTHIANS 1:10-2:5

[God] is the source of your life in Christ Jesus....
Therefore, as it is written, "Let the one who boasts, boast in the Lord."

1 CORINTHIANS 1:30-31

Like many churches today, the church to which Paul wrote the book of 1 Corinthians was dealing with relational problems among its members. Paul said, "There are quarrels among you.... What I mean is that each one of you says, 'I follow Paul,' or 'I follow Apollos,' or 'I follow Cephas,' or 'I follow Christ'" (1:11–12). The schisms which Paul had in view were more than mere disagreements. The term *quarrel* refers to a conflict resulting from rivalry and discord. These divisions stemmed from a selfish spirit of arrogance that is characteristic of unbelievers (it is the same word translated *strife* in Romans 1:29 and Galatians 5:20). The Corinthians were competitive and jealous (1 Corinthians 3:3)—wanting to be more recognized, more liked, and more esteemed than others.

That spirit of rivalry and arrogance is at the core of both the Christian's indwelling sin and the church's ongoing conflict. In fact, the jealous quarrels described in 1 Corinthians were typical in almost every church in the New Testament. Relational problems between Jews and Gentiles seem to be the backdrop of Paul's letter to the Romans. There is considerable emphasis on how to deal with relational conflict in Ephesians 4, Philippians 2, Colossians 3, Philemon, James 4, 1 Peter 1 and 3, and 1 John 3-4. So it shouldn't surprise us that most churches today—even good churches—continue to struggle with relational conflicts between believers.

So how does Paul teach us to deal with our relational conflicts? By pointing us to the Gospel. In 1:18–2:5 he says, in essence, that (1) the Gospel message itself, (2) those whom God chooses to receive it, and (3) the method in which it is preached are all designed to crush human pride. Here's another way of saying it: The Gospel is not something to be arrogant about because the news of a crucified Messiah is a culturally absurd message, received by culturally despised people, and communicated in a culturally unimpressive way. And again: The message is considered foolishness; most of those who receive it are nobodies; and those who are teaching it are unimpressive speakers. Paul's point? *"What in the world are you bragging about?!"*

Pride is the root cause of our conflicts with others, and the Gospel solves those conflicts by crushing our pride. This passage demands that we stop and ask ourselves, "Has the Gospel message percolated long enough in my heart to humble me and crush my arrogance toward other believers?" If you find selfishness, bitterness, and jealousy in your heart today (and most of us do), preach the Gospel to yourself again. And don't stop preaching to yourself until you can say, "The only thing I can boast in is the Lord."

Let the Gospel affect your relationships. —JOE

Imperishable Beauty
READ 1 TIMOTHY 4

Charm is deceitful, and beauty is vain,
but a woman who fears the LORD is to be praised.

PROVERBS 31:30

I'll never forget the funeral of Shirley Oswald, an aged and godly sister in Christ I met early on in my ministry. I didn't meet her until the final few years of her life. She was beyond petite. She was frail from years of illnesses and disease. There was nothing attractive about her appearance. Her body had been afflicted, and it showed. Nevertheless, her eyes shone and her lips smiled, evidencing the love for Christ about which her tongue ceaselessly spoke. Her beauty was spiritual, not physical.

Shirley's funeral was a time of celebration rather than grief. She had worshipped Jesus from afar, and we rejoiced that she was finally worshipping Him face to face. Victory! What I'll not forget, however, was the picture that stood next to the coffin, a picture of Shirley from half a century before I'd met her. She must have been in her twenties at the time, and she was knock-you-back gorgeous. She looked like a movie star from the black-and-white film days. Her skin was flawless, not wrinkled. Her hair was full and beautifully styled, not thin and wiry. Her back was straight, not hunched.

At one time, Shirley Oswald was physically beautiful. That beauty faded, as it will for all of us, despite our efforts to stop the hands of time. Thankfully, however, Shirley had a more important and more enduring beauty—one that time couldn't touch. She had prioritized the health and vitality of her character, not just her body. She had worked to have a tender heart, not just tender hands. She took care to have a pure conscience, not just a clear complexion. Her life had been centered on Christ, and it was full. The Gospel had produced in her an eternal beauty. I rejoiced that day, and I was mindful of several verses which she knew well and which I advise you to consider:

"Charm is deceitful, and beauty is vain, but a woman who fears the LORD is to be praised" (Proverbs 31:30).

"Do not let your adorning be [merely] external—the braiding of hair and the putting on of gold jewelry, or the clothing you wear— but let your adorning be the hidden person of the heart with the imperishable beauty of a gentle and quiet spirit, which in God's sight is very precious" (1 Peter 3:3-4).

"So we do not lose heart. Though our outer self is wasting away, our inner self is being renewed day by day" (2 Corinthians 4:16).

"Rather train yourself for godliness; for while bodily training is of some value, godliness is of value in every way, as it holds promise for the present life and also for the life to come" (1 Timothy 4:7b-8).

Physical beauty is a gift from God, and ladies should endeavor to present themselves attractively. Still, a lady whose main beauty is spiritual is to be praised (Proverbs 31:30). God Himself prizes her (1 Peter 3:4). With that in mind, pursue beauty that is more than skin deep—the "imperishable beauty of a gentle and quiet spirit" (1 Peter 3:4).

Let the Gospel affect your concept of beauty. —CHRIS

The Advantages of Singleness

The unmarried or betrothed woman is anxious about the things of the Lord....
But the married woman is anxious about worldly things,
how to please her husband.

1 CORINTHIANS 7:34

Singleness can be one of the most challenging trials of life. For many, it's a time of insecurity, loneliness, and seemingly unanswered prayers. However, most single believers (and most married believers) fail to consider the advantages of singleness and fail to value it like God does.

Although Paul certainly allowed for single or widowed Christians to marry (7:28, 39; 9:5—in fact, he said in 1 Timothy 4:1-3 that it was "a demonic teaching" to forbid marriage), he preferred and recommended singleness (7:7, 8, 26, 32, 38, 40). He said that a life without marital obligations was good, that he wished all people were single like himself, and that an unmarried woman would be happier if she remained unmarried! Such thinking certainly runs counter to our typical mindset.

Knowing that Paul treasured his Gospel partnership with a married couple like Aquila and Priscilla (Romans 16:3; 1 Corinthians 16:19), and knowing that he used marriage as a picture of the deep mystery of the Gospel (Ephesians 5:22-33), how do we make sense of his strong preference for singleness? Paul preferred singleness for two primary reasons. First, living as a single person was the best way of handling "the present distress" (7:26, 28). This probably refers to the persecution that Gospel-believers were sure to face in Paul's day. Living for the Gospel has rarely been safe. Consider all the distress that Paul endured and how his ministry would have been limited had he been concerned with providing for and protecting a wife and children. Second, living as a single person removes distractions as we serve the Lord (7:29-35). Again, this doesn't mean that married people can't minister. Rather, it means that there are significant advantages in the Gospel ministry of singles, such as more time, more flexibility, and fewer expenses.

Paul's high view of singleness should have three immediate effects. First, if you are still single, you should ask yourself, "Does the Lord desire me to remain single? Is this how I could best use my life for the advance of the Gospel?" Don't assume a negative answer. Craig Blomberg asks, "How often do Christians contemplating getting married ask the question of whether a prospective partner will enable them to serve the Lord better? If they cannot realistically imagine ways in which this could happen, they are probably not ready to 'tie the knot'" (*From Pentecost to Patmos*, 179).

Second, the Bible's esteem of singleness should inspire contentment. Rather than viewing it as a trap from which to escape, see your singleness as God's good and sovereign plan for your life—at least at present. The reality is, if your communion with Christ isn't satisfying your soul now, it won't after marriage, either. Marriage isn't the goal of life, Jane Austen novels notwithstanding. No husband will give the security and fulfillment that comes from Christ alone.

Finally, Paul's teaching on singleness should change the church's mindset toward the unwed. Married believers must be careful not to treat singles as "second class citizens" or "spare tires." They should value and encourage the vital role that singles can play in Christ's church. If someone is gifted with singleness and able to serve the Lord without distraction, then perhaps those who are *married* are the "second class citizens!" In short, we must value the gift of singleness as greatly as God does.

Let the Gospel affect your appreciation of singleness and Christian singles. —JOE

The God-Breathed, Life-Changing Word

READ 2 TIMOTHY 3 & PSALM 19:7–11

*From childhood you have been acquainted with the sacred writings,
which are able to make you wise for salvation through faith in Christ Jesus.
All Scripture is breathed out by God and profitable....*

2 TIMOTHY 3:15-16

Second Timothy, the last known letter which the Apostle Paul wrote, contains several ominous warnings. Chapter 3 begins by noting that there will be "times of difficulty," what the KJV with which I grew up calls "perilous times." Paul spends verses 2–9 of the chapter describing the very sins that are prevalent in our day. It reads like a modern newspaper, in fact. He concludes this dark portion of the chapter by warning that godly people should expect persecution (3:12) and that evil people will get progressively worse as time goes on, not better (3:13).

How, then, should Christians respond to these uniquely precarious times? How can Christians survive when the world is "going to hell in a handbasket?" Paul's answer is instructive, and it's anything but imaginative: "Continue in what you've learned" (3:14). Timothy didn't need something new, and neither do we. He needed to continue in the Scriptures that had been part of his life from infancy (3:14-17). Why?

Because only the Scriptures are the key to our salvation. In verse 15 Paul tells Timothy that the Scriptures which he had been taught by his godly grandmother and mother even while in his highchair "are able to make you wise for salvation through faith in Christ Jesus." There is no substitute. Only the Bible, in which we read of the person and work of Jesus Christ, can teach us of our need to trust Him as the only hope of salvation. (By the way, I can't think of a more hope-giving text for single mothers or mothers married to an unsaved man! Teach your little "Timothys" the soul-saving truth of the Bible!)

Because only the Scriptures are the key to our spiritual growth. Paul goes on in verse 16 to tell of the Bible's divine origin and authority ("all Scripture is breathed out by God") and of its practical, life-changing power ("all Scripture …is profitable"). The two points are intimately connected: The Bible is helpful for teaching, reproving, correcting, and training in righteousness (or, producing spiritual growth) *precisely because* it is breathed out by God and is not merely the collected wisdom of men. Studying the Scriptures is the God-ordained way by which Christians grow in Christlikeness (2 Corinthians 3:18).

Because only the Scriptures are the key to our ministry. Spiritual growth isn't an end in itself. Paul concludes the chapter in verse 17 by saying that the Bible makes Christians mature and well-prepared for spiritual service. So we grow in Christ not merely for our own sakes, but that we might minister well to others.

Only the Bible can do these amazing things. Thus, the way Christians respond to ever-increasing wickedness is to increase our commitment to the Scriptures—not just in theory, but in everyday life. Like Timothy, we need to make the Bible central in our lives: reading it every day; memorizing it; meditating on it; singing it; joining a church that preaches it (2 Timothy 4:2); speaking of it; making it very much "at home" in us (Colossians 3:16). Get into the Word, not out of guilt, but because it's the source of your spiritual life and nourishment!

Let the Gospel affect your Bible study. —CHRIS

Christ Died for Sinners

READ 1 CORINTHIANS 15:1–11

*Now I would remind you, brothers [and sisters], of the gospel
…that Christ died for our sins in accordance with the Scriptures.*

1 CORINTHIANS 15:1-3

What is the Gospel? I've asked this question to many Christians and non-Christians, and it's a bit surprising to discover how many *Christians* have difficulty answering it, even though it's one of life's most crucial matters. Throughout this booklet we urge readers, "Let the Gospel affect your everyday life." This requires that we understand the Gospel, the good news. First Corinthians 15:3-5 gives the most succinct explanation of the Gospel in all the Bible.

You'll notice four *thats* in these verses: "*That* Christ died…*that* he was buried…*that* he was raised…and *that* he appeared." Each of them signals one of four monumental facts: Jesus' death, burial, resurrection, and appearances. The second and fourth events serve to prove the historical reality of the first and third. In other words, the burial proves that He was dead; the six appearances (15:5-8) prove that He came back to life. Because this letter to the Corinthian church was written within 25 years of the events themselves, most of the hundreds of people who witnessed Jesus' actual resurrection were "still alive" (15:6) as Paul penned this letter.

Since Jesus' burial proved His death and His appearances proved His resurrection, the two central events of the Gospel—and of all of human history—are the death and resurrection of Jesus Christ. And Paul says that both were "in accordance with the Scriptures." In other words, Jesus' death and resurrection weren't random events, but were prophesied hundreds of years earlier in the Old Testament (for example, Psalms 2, 16, 22, and Isaiah 53). They were central to God's plan for all of creation.

Although this passage is doctrinal and historical, it's also extremely personal. When Paul explained the death of Jesus, he said, "Christ died *for our sins.*" This is the most basic, most central teaching of the Bible: Jesus died as our substitute. Because we have broken God's laws, we are justly condemned to die for our offenses. However, when Jesus was crucified, He was dying for our sins, taking our punishment on Himself. And when He rose again three days later, He was proving that He had both paid sin's penalty in full and conquered its consequences.

Do these Gospel facts automatically save everyone in the world from eternal condemnation in hell? Not at all. Although Jesus' death for sin is available to all, it is only effective for those who *receive* this message (15:1), who *stand firm* in it (15:1), who *hold fast* to it (15:2), who *believe* it (15:11). These are four different ways of saying the same thing: the only ones who are saved from sin's punishment are those who perseveringly believe in Jesus' death and resurrection. If you have never believed the Gospel, I urge you to trust Christ now. And if you've already believed, I urge you to keep the Gospel "of first importance" in your life (15:3). C. J. Mahaney articulates this so clearly:

> *"If there's anything in life that we should be passionate about, it's the gospel. And I don't mean passionate only about sharing it with others. I mean passionate in thinking about it, dwelling on it, rejoicing in it, allowing it to color the way we look at the world. Only one thing can be of first importance to each of us. And only the gospel ought to be"* (The Cross Centered Life, 20-21).

Let the Gospel be your first priority. —JOE

Praying in Jesus' Name

*Truly, truly, I say to you, whatever you ask of the Father in my name,
he will give it to you.*

JOHN 16:23

Most Christians use the phrase "in Jesus' name" merely as a sanctified sign-off to their prayers. The phrase as many use it might rightly be translated in any number of ways: "Sincerely," or "Ten-four; over-and-out," or "I'm done; it's someone else's turn."

Although this may be a comical exaggeration, it contains a truth that is no laughing matter: we have taken what Jesus provided as a great privilege backed by glorious truths and turned it into a mindless phrase—the very sort of vain repetition which He explicitly forbade (Matthew 6:7). We treat the phrase like so many magic words, and we get offended when someone closes a prayer with a simple "Amen." We're missing the point!

When, the night before His betrayal and crucifixion, Jesus urged the disciples to pray in His name, the central lesson He intended to teach is that *we have access into the presence of the Father on the merits of Jesus Christ* (John 14:13–14; 15:16; 16:23–24, 26). The point is not that we must say the right words or that we'll get everything for which we ask (sometimes, in God's wisdom, we won't!), but that we have an audience with God the Father because of our union with God the Son. And that's far more valuable than any other answer to prayer! Hebrews 10:19–22 puts it this way:

> *"Therefore, brothers, since we have confidence to enter the holy places by the blood of Jesus, by the new and living way that he opened for us through the curtain, that is, through his flesh, and since we have a great priest over the house of God, let us draw near with a true heart in full assurance of faith. . . ."*

The point of praying in Jesus' name is that we are able to claim the privilege of communion with God which rightly belongs to Christ alone. The Father hears us like He hears the Son! We are allowed to "come boldly to the throne of grace" (Hebrews 4:14–16) because of the *righteousness* of Christ credited to us, the *blood* of Christ shed for us, and the *high priesthood* of Christ whereby He represents us. We're not welcomed by God because we've "been good," nor are we excluded because we've "been bad." We're welcomed because of Christ! Understanding this is the key not only to effective prayer, but to the entire Christian life.

Here's a practical suggestion, then. Rather than ending your prayers with a habitual sign-off, *start* your prayers in Jesus' name! Remind yourself of your acceptance through Christ and confess to God these great truths:

> *"Father, I'm not approaching You because of any righteousness of my own, for I have none. I'm painfully aware of my sin. I have no right to be heard by You. Nevertheless, I come, and I do so boldly and gratefully because of the blood and righteousness of your Son. He is worthy to commune with You, and He has granted to me that same privilege. So I pray 'in Jesus' name,' rejoicing in my salvation through Christ."*

Let the Gospel affect your confidence in prayer. —CHRIS

Trusting God in Tough Times
READ PSALM 46

God is our refuge and strength, a very present help in trouble.

PSALM 46:1

Worry is the besetting sin of many believers. We worry about our children, our health, our finances, our government, and our relationships. And as if life weren't complicated enough, many Christians add to the legitimate hardships of life any number of imagined threats and conspiracy theories. Stress is what we do best, it seems. Though we claim to believe in the God of the Bible, we worry like practical atheists.

Unbelief and anxiety aren't new problems, of course. Lack of faith was the besetting sin of God's people throughout the Old Testament. The Patriarchs lied and schemed because they doubted God. The Israelites refused to enter into the Promised Land because they doubted God. Israel and Judah sought protection against enemies from pagan countries and their idols because they doubted God. No wonder Scripture so often commanded them (and commands us) to "fear not."

The Psalms are a great remedy for doubt. They are faith-building songs of worship. They deal honestly with the hardships of life, often expressing the fears and frustrations of their human authors. Yet, they also magnify God's faithfulness and power, especially in the midst of human need. Sometimes they show the journey of the believer from fear to faith, as in Psalm 73. Other times they encourage faith by showing its doctrinal basis, reminding us of truths about God that make trusting Him reasonable and doubting Him ridiculous. That's what Psalm 46 does.

Throughout Psalm 46, the writer acknowledges that life can be tragically difficult. There are times of trouble (46:1). There are occasions when it seems like the whole world is falling apart, pictured by such universal calamities as mountains being thrown into the sea (46:2-3). Add to such natural disasters the depravity of sinners which the calamities symbolize in the psalm. Unbelievers rage against God and the godly (46:6). There are brutal wars on the earth (46:9). The psalmist doesn't offer naïve optimism.

Nevertheless, the sovereignty of God—His absolute authority and control over all things—is even more real to the psalmist than suffering. He begins the psalm with a bold proclamation about God: "God is our refuge and strength, a very present help in trouble" (46:1). What a beautiful and encouraging description, encompassing both His infinite power and His tender compassion. As our *refuge*, God hides us from harm. As our *strength*, He overcomes our frailty. As our *very present help*, He holds our hand and helps us through trouble. He's never absent, and He's never passive. The result of meditating on God's protective care for us is strengthened faith: "Therefore [because of the truths in verse 1] we will not fear" (46:2).

The rest of the Psalm continues the theme of God's sovereign care for His people. He offers peace through conflict today and peace from conflict in the future (46:4-5). He rules rebellious nations today and will silence them in the future (46:6, 8-10). The song's refrain twice rejoices that God protects us like a mighty warrior ("the LORD of Armies") and like a fortress (46:7, 11). Most amazingly of all, it points us to Jesus Christ as the perfect fulfillment of the psalm—the one who is always with us, who gives peace in the midst of storms or even calms them, who will one day conquer the wicked, and who turns us from being God's foes to being His children. *Christ* is the ultimate refuge, strength, and help, and *Christ* is the ultimate dispeller of our fears.

Are you prone to fear? Look Christ-ward. Meditating on God's sovereignty and goodness—especially as displayed through Jesus' death in our place—is the death-blow to doubt.

Let the Gospel increase your faith. —CHRIS

God Compares Himself to a Mother

READ PSALM 131

Can a woman forget her nursing child,
that she should have no compassion on the son of her womb?
Even these may forget, yet I will not forget you.

ISAIAH 49:15

Throughout the Bible, God is almost always referred to with masculine nouns and pronouns. He consistently reveals Himself as Father rather than Mother, King rather than Queen, Shepherd rather than Shepherdess, and Husband rather than Wife. However, there are a few occasions when He reveals the greatness of His love by comparing Himself to a mother. (Paul does the same thing in Galatians 4:19 and 1 Thessalonians 2:7.) Three of these are found toward the end of Isaiah.

"Listen to me, O house of Jacob, all the remnant of the house of Israel, who have been borne by me from before your birth, carried from the womb; even to your old age I am he, and to gray hairs I will carry you. I have made, and I will bear; I will carry and will save" (Isaiah 46:3-4).

In confronting her idolatry, the Lord calls Israel to consider His uniqueness. He is unrivaled in His mother-like relationship to Israel. God is saying in essence, "There is only one woman who is your mother. There is only one person who carried you in the womb for nine months, and went through the travail of labor and delivery for you. I, the Lord, am like that to you."

"But Zion said, 'The LORD has forsaken me; my Lord has forgotten me.' Can a woman forget her nursing child, that she should have no compassion on the son of her womb? Even these may forget, yet I will not forget you" (Isaiah 49:14-15).

In chapter 49, the Lord declares that He will certainly save His people through His Servant, a prophecy of the Lord Jesus. He communicates that He has not forgotten His people with the most powerful illustration—a nursing mother. The Lord is even more attentive to His people than a mother is to her nursing child.

"For thus says the LORD: 'Behold, I will extend peace to her like a river, and the glory of the nations like an overflowing stream; and you shall nurse, you shall be carried upon her hip, and bounced upon her knees. As one whom his mother comforts, so I will comfort you; you shall be comforted in Jerusalem' (Isaiah 66:12-13).

We can all imagine a well-fed baby, bouncing on his mother's knee, laughing with glee as she plays peek-a-boo with him. That is the picture God draws to communicate how He will bless Jerusalem.

Believer, do you realize that God loves you more than a mother loves the child she carried for nine months? Do you believe that God is committed to you more than a mother is committed to her nursing child? Are you confident that God will forever bless you with joy just like a mother plays with and comforts her infant? Mothers, think about the love that you have shown for your children. Now, let that give you a teeny-tiny glimpse of the greatness of God's love for a sinner like you.

Let the Gospel remind you of God's great love. —JOE

Sanctification by Satisfaction
READ PSALMS 23 & 73

Whom have I in heaven but you?
And there is nothing on earth that I desire besides you.

PSALM 73:25

We all know what it's like to be so full after a large dinner that even the most enticing desserts no longer tempt us. In such circumstances, we'll often sigh, touch our stomachs, and decline dessert by telling our hostess, "I'm so full I couldn't eat another bite." Such fullness is a key to avoiding temptation in the Christian life, as well.

Throughout the Scriptures we learn that fellowship with God is a delight. Walking with God is such a pleasure that other joys pale in comparison. Although many people think of Christianity in terms of sacrifice, Scripture describes it in terms of satisfaction, and even pleasure! Rather than being restrained by a spiritual straightjacket lest you do tempting things you wish you could, Scripture describes the Christian life as the source of such great joy that temptations lose their appeal. Like the feeling we have after Thanksgiving dinner, we should be so full of Christ that we don't have room for sin! Consider these verses in that light:

"You make known to me the path of life; in your presence there is fullness of joy; at your right hand are pleasures forevermore" (Psalm 16:11).

"The Lord is my shepherd; I shall not want [or, I lack nothing]" (Psalm 23:1).

"Whom have I in heaven but you? And there is nothing on earth that I desire besides you" (Psalm 73:25).

Does obeying Christ mean saying no to sinful pleasures? Sure. However, saying no to sin in favor of Christ is like saying no to a scooter in favor of a sports car, or no to peanuts in favor of filet mignon. Life with Christ is a feast, not a famine. (There's a thought that should drastically change your view of Christianity!) There is more pleasure in Christ than in sin, and remembering this weakens sin's appeal. Matthew Henry and John Piper concur:

"The joy of the Lord will arm us against the assaults of our spiritual enemies and put our mouths out of taste for those pleasures with which the tempter baits his hooks" (Matthew Henry's commentary on Nehemiah 8:10).

"I know of no other way to triumph over sin long-term than to gain a distaste for it because of a superior satisfaction in God." (John Piper, Desiring God, 12).

These are no empty words. Tracy, a lady whom I was privileged to pastor, found in them (and an extended personal study in Ecclesiastes) deliverance from decades of alcohol abuse. Her joy-inspired victory culminated during a temptation in front of the beer case at a local grocery store. Tracy later called me and told how she had stood in the aisle looking at the beer, but quoting verses that reminded her that Christ is more desirable and satisfying than sin. She nearly wept with exultation when she told me "PC, I walked out of the store without the beer!" Rejoicing in Christ took the teeth out of her temptation. It will do the same for you, whatever your temptation may be. Run from sin by running to Christ! Seek deliverance not in will power or legalistic rules, but in the Savior who died and rose again "to save His people from their sins" (Matthew 1:21).

Let the Gospel affect your battles against temptation. —CHRIS

The LORD God said to the serpent,
"...He shall bruise your head, and you shall bruise his heel."
GENESIS 3:14–15

The creation account in Genesis 1 is cosmic and awe-inspiring. By comparison, the creation account in Genesis 2 is intimate and inviting. Even the name by which God is called changes in 2:4 from "God" (*Elohim*) to "the LORD God" (*Yahweh Elohim*) in 2:5. *Yahweh* (represented in English versions by the capitalized word LORD) is God's personal, covenant name.

Genesis 2 highlights Yahweh's amazing goodness to Adam and Eve. The Garden of Eden was a place of perfect beauty. *Eden* (which is a Hebrew term) means *pleasure*. The trees were bountiful. The climate was tropical, with daily mist and not one drop of rain. The rivers were therefore not rain-fed, but spring-fed. Even the rocks were valuable (2:11–12)! This was the greatest of all resorts, and the entire scene demonstrated God's amazing love and goodness toward Adam and Eve.

God further displayed His goodness by giving Adam the perfect lifestyle. He had the perfect job, cultivating the garden in a world without weeds. He simply had to channel the growth of perfect plants in a perfect climate! God also gave him amazing provision and freedom. Adam could eat of every tree in the garden except one. Even this one prohibition gave Adam the opportunity to evidence his love for and trust in his Maker. God showed even more goodness by creating for Adam a wife that was "a helper corresponding to him" (2:18) Eve was the perfect complement and companion!

The last and most significant display of God's goodness was His own presence with Adam and Eve in the garden (3:8). The Lord Jesus Christ, who would one day be the seed of the woman (3:15), walked with Adam and Eve. They were privileged with personal, daily, unhindered fellowship with Jesus. Imagine that—the first Adam and "the last Adam" (1 Corinthians 15:45) in close fellowship, long before Christ would die to repair the damages Adam's sin incurred!

Despite all of His goodness toward them, Adam and Eve chose to disobey God (3:6). In consequence, God cursed Eve and all women after her by decreeing that they would have pain in childbirth (including all of its associated functions, like menstruation and menopause) and a natural inclination to "dominate" their husbands (3:16). He cursed Adam and all men after him with a lifetime of toilsome labor and the certain reality of death (3:17–19). Nevertheless, God was good even when He cursed them! Even *before* God ever cursed Adam and Ever for their sin, He promised to obliterate Satan's existence and influence through the Lord Jesus (3:15). Eve's descendant would completely crush Satan, while enduring only a temporary bruise in the conflict. This was and is the greatest display of God's goodness—His eternal purpose to send His Son to die for those who spurned His goodness!

Right now, we are living between the two comings of Christ. However, the outcome of the battle is not "up for grabs." Jesus has already won the victory at the cross and the tomb. So even though we continue to struggle, to sin, and to grieve, we can have unshakable confidence that God is only good and that Jesus is coming soon to (merely) "finish the job."

Let the Gospel affect your perspective on the brokenness all around you. —JOE

Gazing on Christ
READ 2 CORINTHIANS 3-4

And we all, with unveiled face, beholding the glory of the Lord,
are being transformed into the same image from one degree of glory to another.
2 CORINTHIANS 3:18

One of the most dangerous lies which Satan has sold to the church is the idea that the person and work of Jesus Christ are the "milk" of Christianity, best suited for the flannelgraphs we show to children or the tracts we give to the unsaved. The truth is that every part of our salvation depends on our relationship with the Lord Jesus!

Scripture teaches that we are justified by looking in faith to Jesus Christ (Isaiah 45:22; John 1:29; 2 Corinthians 4:4-6). Justification is what we generally mean when we speak of someone being "saved." It is God's declaring the guilty sinner to be righteous. The basis of justification is the work of Christ—His righteous life which is credited to the sinner, and His penal death in place of the sinner, whose sins have been credited to Him. The trigger of justification is faith in Christ. We are "justified by faith" (Romans 3:28; 5:1).

Scripture further teaches that we are sanctified by looking in faith to Jesus Christ (2 Corinthians 3:18). In Scripture, sanctification often describes our growth in holiness. We're justified the moment we trust Christ, but we're sanctified progressively throughout the rest of our lives. 2 Corinthians 3:18 says that we grow to be like Christ as we study Him in the Scriptures. So our growth isn't dependent on special strategies or spiritual tricks. Instead, it takes place as we worshipfully study the Lord Jesus through the Word, day by day.

Finally, Scripture teaches that we will be glorified by looking on Jesus when our lives on earth are finished. When we see Him in all of His glory, we will be like Him—glorified and sinless (1 John 3:2). What a day that will be! "Come, Lord Jesus!"

Thus, your life as a believer begins (justification), continues (sanctification), and culminates (glorification) by looking to Jesus Christ. You never get over Him or what He has done to you. The goal and thrill of your life should be to "Behold the Lamb of God who takes away the sins of the world" (John 1:29b). Gaze on Jesus Christ!

We have looked in faith to Christ, beholding God's atoning Lamb.
He for our sins was sacrificed; thus we, though dead, have been born again.

We still look each day to Christ and by the unveiled view are changed.
The Spirit wields the Truth with might, conforming us to the Son unstained.

We will look one day on Christ when He appears, triumphantly.
That blessed hope now purifies, till seeing Him, we like Him will be.

Jesus, Your beauty fills our eyes—first looking, we were justified;
Now gazing deeper sanctifies, till face to face, we are glorified.

"Your Beauty Fills Our Eyes" by Chris Anderson and Greg Habegger

Let the Gospel affect your worship. —CHRIS

The Two Shall Be One Flesh

READ EPHESIANS 5:22–33

Therefore a man shall leave his father and his mother and hold fast to his wife, and they shall become one flesh.

GENESIS 2:24

Genesis 2:24 is God's inspired blueprint for marriage. It is quoted by Malachi (Malachi 2:15), Paul (1 Corinthians 6:16; Ephesians 5:31), and Christ (Matthew 19:4–6) as the authoritative word on the marriage relationship. Notice how it was cited both before and after the fall and in both testaments. It's loaded with lessons for a unified marriage.

First, the husband and wife are one in their commitment to one another. God's plan for marriage begins by prioritizing the marriage relationship over all other human relationships. The husband (and the wife, implicitly) are to "leave" their parents and "cleave" (or "hold fast") to one another. That means that there should be no one more important to you than your husband, including your friends, your parents, and even your children.

Second, the husband and wife are one in their aspirations. Although you'll each have unique hobbies and interests, your oneness should be evident in mutual goals, friends, celebrations, and sorrows. You should no longer think in terms of *my* (as in my paycheck, my savings, my vacation, my car, my goals), but in terms of *our.*

Third, the husband and wife are one in their physical love. Although the one-flesh relationship is much more than physical intimacy, it does include it, and it is expressed beautifully in this God-blessed way. Adam and Eve were presented to each other without clothing and without shame, and they were commanded to engage in sexual intimacy (Genesis 1:28). That command is repeated throughout the Scriptures (Proverbs 5:15-19; 1 Corinthians 7:1-5).

Fourth, the husband and wife are one in their worship and ministry. When Adam and Eve's relationship was right, it included frequent walks with God—as a couple—in Eden. God created married couples to enjoy fellowship with Him together. They are fellow heirs as Christians (1 Peter 3:7), and they are to worship and serve Him together (exemplified by Aquila and Priscilla in Acts 18).

Of course, we all know that the ideal for marriage described in Genesis 2 is unattainable for sinners like us. The title of Dave Harvey's helpful book nails it: problems are inevitable *When Sinners Say "I Do."* Marriage can reveal our innate selfishness more than any other relationship. Thankfully, the Scriptures give us not only a blueprint for marriage, but also a remedy for the times when we ignore God's plan. The hope for sinners, married or single, is the Gospel. It provides Christ's righteousness to us. It enables our obedience. And when we still blow it—and we will—it provides forgiveness through Christ (1 John 2:1-2) and enables us to forgive one another (Ephesians 4:32). Successful husbands and wives are those who perpetually extend to one another the grace which they've received through Christ—*sinners forgiving sinners.* And that's essential in light of one last point from Genesis 2:24…

The husband and wife are one indissolubly. When Christ quoted Genesis 2:24 in Matthew 19:4-6, He insisted that the union between a man and a woman is made by God and is therefore permanent. "What therefore God has joined together, let not man put asunder" is a divine imperative, not just a pious-sounding line invented by pastors for Christian weddings.

According to Genesis 2:24, the husband and wife *are* one flesh. That's a fact, not just a goal. By God's grace, and with absolute dependence on the Gospel, determine to live like it.

Let the Gospel affect your marriage. —CHRIS

Jesus' Crucifixion & My Trials

READ ROMANS 5:1-11

We rejoice in our sufferings....
For while we were still weak, at the right time Christ died for the ungodly.

ROMANS 5:3, 6

Life is filled with disappointments and hardships. Responding to them in a Christian manner is a constant challenge. Since thinking "Christianly" means thinking biblically, you'll find great hope from Romans 5 when troubles come.

It's important to note that Romans 5:1 is a bridge from one section of this letter to the next. Chapters 1-4 explain how "we are justified [declared to be righteous in God's sight] by faith" (5:1a), whereas chapters 5-8 unpack the benefits of those who are justified. In particular, the first eleven verses of Romans 5 are all about how the work of Jesus on the cross drastically alters our standing, state of mind, and security—each of which affects how we respond to our trials.

First, the Gospel changes our standing: We are reconciled. Our reconciled relationship with God is mentioned four times in this paragraph. Paul starts by informing us in verse 1 that "we have peace with God through our Lord Jesus Christ." He continues in verse 2: "Through [Jesus Christ] we have also obtained access by faith into this grace in which we stand." Here he paints a vivid picture, saying that we now have access to and even live in the land of *Grace*, a country in which we will forever enjoy God's favor, though we deserve the exact opposite. In verse 10, Paul again notes that "we were reconciled to God by the death of his Son." He wraps up the topic in verse 11: "through [Jesus Christ] we have now received reconciliation." Notice how each statement emphasizes the fact that we who were God's enemies because of our sin now have peace with Him because of Jesus' death.

Second, the Gospel changes our state of mind: We boast. The word *boast* occurs three times in these eleven verses, although the ESV translates it *rejoice* each time. The mindset Paul has in mind is not simply joyful; it's exuberantly and abundantly confident! Paul says in verse 2 that "we boast in hope of the glory of God" (5:2). This means that we, as reconciled sinners, should be almost brash in our certainty that we will see and experience the glory, beauty and majesty of God for all eternity. He continues in verse 3, noting that our boasting isn't relegated to the future or to ideal circumstances: "we boast in our sufferings." (We'll discuss verse 3 below.) Paul takes up the theme again in verse 11: "We also boast in God through our Lord Jesus Christ." Together, these verses insist that, even through trials, the dominant mood of your life should be positive rather than negative, optimistic rather than pessimistic, confident rather than insecure, marked by indomitable joy rather than persistent gloom. Why? Because of what God has done for you through Jesus.

Third, the Gospel changes our security: We hope. Notice the progression in verses 3 and 4. In the end, sufferings produce in us a hope—a certain expectation—that will never let us down. On what basis? How can Christians remain joyful in the midst of disease, weariness, financial struggles, and relational conflicts? Because the Holy Spirit has deluged our hearts with the love of God (5:5). Because we were God's enemies when Jesus died to demonstrate God's love for us (5:6-8). And because we are certain that we will never face God's wrath (5:9-10). So go ahead, Christian, *boast* in your sufferings, mindful that Jesus' death for you changes everything!

Let the Gospel affect your mindset toward trials. —JOE

Extravagant Worship
READ MARK 14:1-26

She has done a beautiful thing to me.

MARK 14:5

Though we are but saved sinners, God takes joy in our worship, especially when it costs us something. In the days preceding Christ's crucifixion, Mary (compare with John 12:1-8) lavished on Him a gift of remarkable sacrifice, anointing His head with an ointment worth about a year's wages—say $40,000 in our day! In a matter of minutes, tens of thousands of dollars were soaked into Jesus' hair, skin, and clothing, then evaporated into the air, never to be reclaimed. What extravagance!

By the disciples' standards, the gift was an outrageous waste. They indignantly scolded Mary for her folly. Sure, Judas was the most outspoken (because he was a thief [John 12:6]), but all of them sided with him against Mary, complaining that the treasure should have been used in a more practical way, perhaps to help the poor (Mark 14:5).

By Mary's standards, the gift was a humble testimony of love. She was more amazed by her Savior than her savings, and more aware of what He had given her than what she was giving Him. F. N. Peloubet describes her actions thus:

"No words could express her feelings. No common deed could tell him how deep was her gratitude, how strong her desire to honor him, how loving her sympathy, how great was her faith in him, as the Messiah, the Redeemer of the world" (Select Notes: A Commentary on the International Lessons for 1906, *303*).

By Jesus' standards, the gift was a beautiful, prophetic, unforgettable act of worship. Christ defended Mary by saying that her lavish gift was beautiful and appropriate (Mark 14:6-9). It was as noble as ministering to the needy. It was preparatory for His death. In a sense Jesus was defending His own worth more than Mary's worship, for the disciples tragically assumed that money spent in His honor was "wasted." What earth-bound thinking! Soon enough Christ's head would be covered with blood and sweat and spit. Soon enough His body would be wrapped for burial. Soon enough He would be absent, and other worthwhile expenditures could be made. But Mary's gift delighted Him, and He promised that it would never be forgotten (Mark 14:9).

Are we not prone to be more like the disciples than like Mary? Don't we want to worship Christ, but avoid "going overboard"; to attend church, but not let it dictate our schedules; to love Jesus, but not talk about Him; to give an occasional offering, but not sacrifice or limit other expenditures? We could learn much from Mary's example.

Consider what the characters' actions reveal about their hearts. Judas was *preoccupied with himself*. Tragically, he responded to Mary's gift to Christ by selling Christ (Mark 14:10). The disciples were *preoccupied with the needy*—a good thing, but not the best thing. But Mary? Mary, here as at other times, was *preoccupied with Christ*, who is more than worthy of our extravagant worship.

Let the Gospel affect your giving. —CHRIS

Grace in the Lives of Ruth & Boaz
READ RUTH 1:1-22 & 4:13-22

All my fellow townsmen know that you are a worthy woman.
RUTH 3:11

Ruth is the main character of the short and engaging book that bears her name. In chapter 1, empty Naomi and loyal Ruth return to Bethlehem because of bitter providence in Moab. In chapter 2, Ruth happens to glean in Boaz's field and finds grace in his eyes. In chapter 3, Ruth seeks security in Boaz with Naomi's counsel. In chapter 4, Boaz acquires Ruth as his wife after approaching the closer relative who had the first right of redemption.

In the end, Ruth, a Gentile who commits herself to the God of Israel, finds nothing but grace! She is blessed by God with a godly husband and a godly heritage—she is the great-grandmother of King David and a direct ancestor of Jesus Christ (Matthew 1:5). Further, she is the living example of "the Proverbs 31 woman." The Hebrew phrase that is translated "a worthy woman" in Ruth 3:11 is identical to the phrase "an excellent wife" in Proverbs 31:10. Also, the book of Ruth immediately follows Proverbs in the Hebrew arrangement of the Old Testament.

There are two questions I'd like to explore for today's meditation, each focusing on the godly examles of Boaz and Ruth.

First, what can explain the amazing grace that Boaz showed to Ruth? Although Boaz could have been standoffish toward Ruth because of her ethnicity, her background, or her bitter mother-in-law, he graciously inquired about her (2:5-7), talked to her (2:8), gave her gleaning privileges (2:8-9), prayed for her (2:12), welcomed her to a meal (2:14), provided her with abundant food (2:15-16), and eventually married her (4:13). Is there anything that can explain his kindness? One probable reason is that Boaz was a great-grandson of Rahab (compare Ruth 4:18-20 with Matthew 1:3-6). One of his relatives was the notorious prostitute from Jericho who found grace when she turned from her sin and trusted in the God of Israel. Boaz must have been aware of God's awesome kindness to his family. Reflecting on God's amazing grace toward you and others in your family will produce in you godly graciousness toward others.

Second, what qualities made Ruth a virtuous woman? In 3:10-11, Boaz mentions two kindnesses that she had shown. Ruth's first kindness was her commitment to Naomi and to Naomi's God. Boaz had previously recognized this kindness in 2:11-12. Ruth's second kindness was that she refused to be flirtatious with the young men in the field. It would have been tempting for a poor women who was gleaning among younger men to use her eyes and body to get their attention and assistance. Ruth was commended, not because she had a perfect past or because she had never sinned, but because she was committed to the Lord and to the godly design of giving herself—soul and body—to one man. Through the grace of God, it is possible for any woman, no matter what her past, to be a virtuous woman. Thus, Ruth is an example not merely of human kindness, but of life-changing grace.

Let the Gospel affect your future, regardless of your past. —JOE

God's Love for Infants Who Die
READ 2 SAMUEL 12:1-23

*"Let the little children come to me and do not hinder them,
for to such belongs the kingdom of heaven."*

MATTHEW 19:14

The death of an infant is a grief that is profoundly painful. It's a trial that is all too common, as I've learned from both my family and my church family. It's also a loss that is never forgotten. Even for those with the most exemplary trust in God, the hurt remains tearfully fresh even after three or four decades.

I've also come to learn that many Christians are ill-prepared to comfort hurting parents. Too often, those who are suffering are given little hope, and careless words only deepen their suffering, much like the hurtful piety of Job's three friends. Frequently this is *because* the Christians have much sound theology. They know that the Bible clearly teaches that life and personhood begin at conception (Genesis 25:22; Job 31:15; Psalm 139:13-16; Jeremiah 1:5; Luke 1:24-44), that every child inherits Adamic guilt (Romans 5:12; Psalm 51:5; 58:3), and that infants are incapable of saving faith (Romans 10:9-10). In view of such realities, is it possible to offer any words of comfort? Can parents grieve in hope? Does the Bible provide any balm for parents whose infant children have died through miscarriage, abortion, still-birth, tragedy, or disease?

There are at least four biblical reasons to believe that infants go to heaven when they die. First, the Scriptures teach that God has special ownership of all children. He calls even the children of unbelievers "my children" (Ezekiel 16:20-21). Second, Jesus evidenced a particular love for children. He taught that the kingdom of heaven belongs to such as them (Matthew 19:14). Ninteenth century Princeton theologian Charles Hodge commented that these words of Jesus seem to indicate that "heaven was in great measure composed of the souls of redeemed infants" (*Systematic Theology*, 1:26-27). Third, although infant children are in fact sinful, God does not view them as worthy of punishment. Instead He views them, in this sense, as innocent (Jeremiah 19:4-5; Jonah 4:11). Finally, David's confidence upon the loss of his infant son—his attitude even more than his words—indicates that he expected to see him again (2 Samuel 12:14-23; contrast this with David's inconsolable grief over the death of his wicked son Absalom in 2 Samuel 18-19).

So the Bible does not teach that only infants who are baptized go to heaven, that only the infant children of believing parents go to heaven, or that some infants are elect and others are not. Rather, the four truths above have lead Christians throughout history to believe that every infant who dies goes immediately into the presence of Jesus Christ in heaven. Charles Spurgeon thus consoled his flock more than a century ago:

> *"Let every mother and father…know assuredly that 'it is well with the child' [2 Kings 4:24] if God hath taken it away from you in its infant day….You may rest assured that it is well with the child, well in a higher and a better sense than it is well with yourselves; well without limitation, well without exception, well infinitely, well eternally."*

Infants, before their births and after, are precious to our Savior. When their lives are tragically or even sinfully taken, Jesus mercifully applies His saving blood to them and welcomes them into His kingdom. God's grace triumphs over both evil and tragedy. Grieving mother, if you know Christ, heaven will be a place of glad reunion; where God's sheer grace in Christ is magnified by all; where God by His untraceable wisdom will bring eternal joy from your deep, but short-lived sorrow.

Let the Gospel help you grieve in hope. —JOE

Hope for the Hopeless
READ JOHN 4

Look, I tell you, lift up your eyes, and see that
the fields are white for harvest.

JOHN 4:35

The Samaritan woman whose conversation with Jesus Christ is recorded in John 4 is one of the more pitiable characters in all of the Scriptures. She had been around the block with several men. She had been married five times, was now "shacked up" with a sixth man, and had probably also had who-knows-how-many other relationships (4:16-18). She was immoral, to be sure, but she was probably also broken and lonely. She was perpetually looking for love and security but was perpetually finding lust and rejection, instead.

Her failed relationships with men probably led to miserable relationships with women. I expect that she was looked down upon as easy and seductive. She was "from the wrong side of the tracks." Thus, it seems, she came to the well by herself, not when other ladies were there working and visiting together. She was an outsider even among her own.

Add to the graveyard's worth of skeletons in her closet the fact that she was a half-breed—a Samaritan, whom Jews despised—and you have a pathetic character. She was used to being ignored and ostracized. No wonder, then, that Jesus' kind words to her caught her by surprise (4:9). Rather than shunning her, giving her a dirty look, or embarrassing her, Jesus started a conversation. More importantly, He directed that conversation to her spiritual needs, offering this tragically thirsty and longing woman *spiritual* refreshment and satisfaction: a drink of living water. He could provide for her a relationship with Himself that would meet all of her spiritual needs, both during her life and throughout eternity (4:10-14).

To cut to the chase, Jesus revealed Himself to the woman as the Christ, the promised Messiah (4:25-26). In so doing, He changed her life. Out of one who was worthless Jesus made a worshiper (4:23-24) and a witness (4:28-30). The Gospel captured her, and through her, her entire community (4:39-42). Where others (including the disciples, apparently [4:27]) saw a sinner to *condemn*, Jesus saw a sinner to *save*. That's what He does, after all. He came to seek and save lost people (Luke 19:10; 5:32). And in context, Jesus' seeking to save this lowly lady and her neighbors is really just another way of saying that God is seeking worshipers (4:23-24). Our Lord doesn't find worshipers; He *makes* them out of notorious sinners through the Gospel!

Do you see yourself in this woman? Are you filled with disappointments? Are you ashamed of your sinful relationships? Are you "worthless" in the eyes of others—and even your own? Christ offers you forgiveness. He offers you lifelong satisfaction. He offers you Himself.

Are you, on the other hand, a lady who tends to ostracize and condemn others for their spiritual needs, social position, or even racial differences? I point *you* to Christ as well, both as the forgiver of your arrogance and as an example of selfless compassion. Where others saw a harlot, Jesus saw a harvest (4:35). May we learn to see people as He does! Indeed, may we learn to see *ourselves* as Samaritan women!

Let the Gospel affect your view of fellow sinners. —CHRIS

Marriage to a Non-Christian Man

READ 1 CORINTHIANS 7:1–24

If any woman has a husband who is an unbeliever,
and he consents to live with her, she should not divorce him.
For the unbelieving husband is made holy because of his wife....
Otherwise your children would be unclean, but as it is, they are holy.

1 CORINTHIANS 7:13-14

Several women in the congregation I pastor are married to men that don't believe in Jesus. This is a very difficult situation. It is encouraging, however, to remember that Christian women found themselves in the same situation two thousand years ago. It's even more encouraging to know that God breathed out words for women who find themselves in this circumstance.

In 1 Corinthians 7:8-16 Paul gives marital counsel to three different groups of believers. First, he advises those believers who have been widowed to remain single if they are able (7:8-9). If they do pursue marriage, Paul later insists that they marry "only in the Lord" (7:39). Second, he commands the believing couples not to divorce (7:10-11). Third, he writes to those who are in "mixed marriages" (a Christian married to a non-Christian) to remain in the marriage if at all possible for the spiritual benefit to the unsaved spouse (7:12-16). We will focus on this last bit of counsel as it applies to Christian wives.

Notice that God commands the believer to remain married to her unbelieving husband as long as the non-Christian consents. Paul gives an absolute command to the believer in this situation: "Do not pursue a divorce" (7:13)! Apparently, some of the Christians in the Corinthian church were using their religious beliefs as a way out of a tough relationship. With the lax divorce laws in our culture, incompatibility of religious conviction would certainly be an easy out. However, Paul forbids believers from thinking that faith in the Gospel can be used as an excuse for divorce.

Why shouldn't the believer pursue a divorce? The answer is given very clearly in verse 14. The Christian must not leave because she has a sanctifying effect on her unbelieving husband and children. The text says, "The unbelieving husband is *made holy* because of his wife." What does that mean? The fact that the unbeliever is *made holy* does not mean that he is saved by association. Rather, the basic meaning of "to make holy" (or "to sanctify"), is "to set apart." In other words, the unbelieving spouse is set apart for the Lord's special attention. And this doesn't apply to your spouse alone; it also applies to your children. As John MacArthur writes, "One Christian in a home graces the entire home" (*First Corinthians*, 166). The unbelieving husband will need to trust Christ on his own to be saved, but he is given the blessing of an around-the-clock Christian influence in his home. (Since this devotional was originally written in early 2009, I've rejoiced with several ladies at the conversion of their husbands. Christianity is contagious, and unsaved men have been "catching it" from their wives. Praise the Lord!)

Christian wife, is this a verse that you treasure? Do you really believe these words? Do you really believe that the God of the universe has set apart your unsaved husband and children for His special attention? Do you really believe that He knows your family by name and has singled out your husband and children? This reality should fan the flame of your faith. It should embolden your prayers for your husband. And it should encourage you to pursue a quiet, winsome godliness (1 Peter 3:1) with a deep sense of God's presence with you and attentiveness to your unbelieving family members.

Let the Gospel increase your commitment to your husband. —JOE

Women & the Passion of Christ

READ MATTHEW 27:33–28:20

There were also many women there, looking on from a distance.

MATTHEW 27:55

Despite the protestations of some, it would be a mistake to think of Christianity as a man's religion. Certainly the Bible affirms the headship of men in the church and in the home. However, the Scriptures also speak of the invaluable ministry of godly women. Indeed, the Bible often records the faithfulness of women even as their male counterparts were failing famously. The record of Christ's passion is one such instance. Christ's male followers failed severely, despite their audacious promises to the contrary (Matthew 27:47-56, 65-75). Judas betrayed Christ. The eleven forsook Christ. Peter, the "president" of the disciples, denied Christ three times. By God's grace, the female disciples fared better.

Godly women were present at Christ's death. Matthew 27:55-56 tells us that many faithful women watched the crucifixion of Jesus from a distance. Surely it was a mournful watch they kept. Yet, Scripture honors them for their fortitude and faithfulness. Perhaps their adoring looks were a comfort to Christ as He hung alone. Perhaps it was dangerous for these women to be present, especially since the crowd of spectators continued to mock the Savior even as He died. It is to the credit of these ladies that they continued with Christ even during His time of unimaginable suffering.

Godly women were present at Christ's burial. Following Jesus' death, His body was prepared for burial by two influential men, Joseph of Arimathea and Nicodemas (Matthew 27:56-60). Again, however, the eleven were conspicuously absent. Nevertheless, Christ's female followers were again present, looking on as their Lord's body was laid in the tomb (Matthew 27:61).

Godly women were present at Christ's resurrection. "Very early" that Sunday morning, Mary Magdalene, Mary the mother of James, and Salome went to the garden tomb with spices intended for Christ's dead body (Matthew 28:1; Mark 16:1-2). They naturally wondered who would roll the stone away (Mark 16:3), for the men were again nowhere to be found. Of course, there would be no anointing of a dead body that day, for Christ had risen! Angels made the announcement and sent the ladies as the first human messengers of Christ's resurrection (Mark 16:4-8). Later, Christ would appear to Mary Magdalene, who was honored as the first to see the resurrected Christ (Mark 16:9; John 20:11-18). Many have wondered why the Lord Jesus appeared first to a lady on that first Easter Sunday morning. Various reasons have been suggested, but perhaps the most obvious is that the male disciples were still cowering in fear days after the crucifixion (John 20:19). Not so the ladies. They honored Christ even when they mistakenly believed that His life and ministry were over.

We should be grateful that the Lord rallied the disciples by His resurrection, forgiveness, and gift of the Spirit (John 20:19-22). And we should earnestly pray for the male leaders of our homes and churches. However, we should also remember that godly ladies played a prominent role in Christ's life, death, and resurrection, just as godly ladies play a prominent role in the life of Christ's church today.

Let the Gospel inspire your faithfulness to Christ. —CHRIS

Godly Romance
READ SONG OF SOLOMON 1–2

Let my beloved come to his garden, and eat its choicest fruits.
SONG OF SOLOMON 4:16

Song of Solomon is among the most neglected books of Scripture. Many Christians have never heard it preached. Yet the very title of the book is actually *The Song of Songs*, which is a Hebrew way of saying "the greatest of all songs." Why is the greatest song in the world about a deeply passionate and pleasurable marriage relationship? First, because marital intimacy is a wonderful thing, ordained and celebrated by God Himself! Second, and deeper, the greatest of all songs is about marriage because marriage pictures the greatest of all stories: Jesus' love for His church. That's not to say that this book is an allegory. It's not. It's about marital intimacy, period. However, marriage itself reflects a greater relationship (Ephesians 5:22-33), as Josh Harris teaches so powerfully:

> *"God didn't get His inspiration for loving the church from marriage. Rather, God created marriage to illustrate His love for the church. God invented romance and pursuit and the promise of undying love between a man and a woman so that throughout our lives we could catch a faint glimmer of the intense love Christ has for those He died to save"* (Stop Dating the Church, 38).

With that in mind, here are ten inspired lessons from Solomon's wife for delighting in sexual intimacy with your husband.

First, take some initiative. And whatever you do, avoid passivity. One of the greatest blessings a wife can give to her husband is initiating intimacy. Solomon's wife did so frequently (1:2, 7; 4:16; 7:11-12; 8:14). **Second,** speak with terms of endearment. In this brief book, Solomon's bride used tender descriptions more than thirty times, calling him "you whom my soul loves," "my beloved," "my love," and "my friend." Marital intimacy is spiritual and emotional, not just physical. **Third,** kindle your imagination. Much of the joy of love is anticipating moments of intimacy (1:2; 2:5; 5:8; 8:1, 14). **Fourth,** share your insecurities. When possible, a wife should be transparent with her husband about her fears, even those regarding her appearance (1:5-6). **Fifth,** enflame your husband's desire with your words. Solomon's wife understood the provocative power of subtlety (4:16), double entendre (8:2), and teasing (1:7-8). She talked about lovemaking almost twice as much as her husband in the book! **Sixth,** accessorize. Notice the power of jewelry (1:10-11; 4:4, 9), perfume (1:3, 12; 4:6, 10-11; 5:5, 13), lingerie (4:11; 6:7), foods (2:5), and fragrances (3:6; 7:13) to enhance the experience of intimacy. **Seventh,** improve your kissing. Suffice it to say that kissing in the Song involves more than a peck on the cheek (4:11; 5:16; 7:9). **Eighth,** compliment your husband's attractiveness. Solomon's wife lavished him with compliments regarding his head, hair, eyes, cheeks, lips, arms, body, legs, and mouth (1:16; 2:9; 5:11-16). Do the same. **Ninth,** reflect on special moments. Remind your husband of your engagement (2:10-13) and wedding (3:6-11). Even take the time to write about special memories and rehearse them to each other. This whole book, after all, is composed of poems written by a married couple about special moments in their marriage. **Tenth,** ask the Lord to give you a greater appreciation for your husband. Solomon's wife showed her esteem by praising him (2:3; 5:10-15).

Seek to deepen your marital romance. It will delight both you and your husband, and it will remind you of the relationship between the Savior and His imperfect but beloved bride.

Let the Gospel affect the romance in your marriage. —JOE

The Fool-Proof Test of Godliness
READ JAMES 1:19-27 & 3:1-18

*If anyone thinks he is religious and does not bridle his tongue
but deceives his heart, this person's religion is worthless.*

JAMES 1:26

Every generation has probably had a tendency to define godliness by a few carefully-chosen "spiritual litmus tests." In our day, we are prone to equate godliness with the way a woman dresses, whether or not she works outside of the home, her listening and viewing habits, and other visible practices. While each of these is worth considering, we must avoid the temptation to prioritize such issues while ignoring other more significant evidences of true spirituality. That's the point of James 1:26: someone who seems (to herself and to others) to be spiritual but doesn't hold her tongue is self-deceived, and her supposed religion is vain. The tongue either proves or disproves a person's genuine godliness.

James 1 goes on to say that true religion is demonstrated by controlling your tongue: avoiding gossip, petty criticism, complaining, and discouraging speech, for example (1:26). Moreover, one whose relationship with the Lord is legitimate not only avoids tearing down others with her tongue, but actively ministers to them (especially widows and orphans) while also keeping herself from being contaminated by the world (1:27).

James 3 continues the epistle's focus on the tongue. The tongue is so important that the ability to control it is indicative of a lady's maturity and of her ability to control the rest of her life (3:2-5a). The tongue is compared to a fire that, if untamed, will lead to the destruction of the entire body in hell (3:5-6). It is full of poison and is virtually impossible to control apart from the power of God (3:7-8). As discussed in James 1:26, the tongue betrays spiritual hypocrisy, sometimes piously praising God, yet viciously tearing apart those whom He has made, including family members (3:9-12). As a spring can't produce both pure and bitter water, and as a tree can't produce two kinds of fruit, so one who at one time professes spirituality and at another unleashes her verbal fury is living a lie. The verbal sins are real and the apparent piety false.

These are hard words, but they are consistent with the entire biblical record. A lady's tongue says a great deal about her heart. The virtuous woman's speech is characterized by wisdom and kindness (Proverbs 31:26), even as the temptress uses her words to entice and flatter (Proverbs 5:3; 7:21). Speech which builds up is one indication of the life changed by Christ, even as corrupt and discouraging speech typifies the unsaved (Ephesians 4:29). Most importantly, our Savior is noted for speech that lacked deception, abuse, or threats (1 Peter 2:22-23). To be like Christ is to bridle our tongues.

No wonder James 1:19 commands us to be quick to hear and slow to speak. Obeying this order isn't easy. In fact, it's impossible apart from the power of the Gospel and the control of the Holy Spirit. Nevertheless, a tamed tongue is an indication of real godliness—much more reliable than, say, whether a lady wears pants or skirts to church.

Let the Gospel affect your speech. —CHRIS

How Moms Talk to Their Sons

READ PROVERBS 31

The words of King Lemuel. An oracle that his mother taught him.

PROVERBS 31:1

Too many of us skip over the opening verse of Proverbs 31 in order to get to "the good stuff," the description of the virtuous woman. In overlooking the introduction, however, we miss two critical matters—the chapter's intended audience and its primary application for women. First, this chapter was not primarily intended to provide an example for women to imitate (though it's certainly a helpful template of godly character). Rather, it was meant to help a son determine which qualities to value as he chose a potential bride. Second, the main thing Proverbs 31 teaches women is how moms should counsel their sons. The chapter highlights the place that mothers have in shepherding their children to make godly choices in life. We dare not overlook the first verse of Proverbs 31. This is part of "the good stuff!"

Although no one is quite certain who King Lemuel was, there's no doubt that Solomon considered the counsel he received to be the most profound and most beautiful piece of motherly advice ever written. It is profound because it deals so directly and succinctly with a king's most destructive enemies: women and wine (31:2-9). It is beautiful because it captures in poetic form the most enduring qualities of a godly wife, whose value is worth more than priceless treasures (31:10-31). Lemuel is urged to value trustworthiness, selflessness, strength, generosity, ingenuity, kindness, and diligence. (Contrary to the perspective of many Christians, the virtuous woman was not "barefoot and pregnant," but was significantly involved in business.) Most importantly, Lemuel's mother taught him to look beyond outward beauty (a quality that most single men put at the top of their "qualifications" list, but which can be deceitful and temporary) and to find a woman who fears the Lord (31:30).

Although she provided excellent instruction, Lemuel's mother also taught him that finding a godly wife was absolutely impossible apart from the grace of God. That is precisely what the phrase, "Who can find?" means (31:10; see also Proverbs 18:22; 19:14). This is a crucial point. Moms, training your children in wisdom is more than training them to make smart decisions. They must learn to rely on God's saving grace, to submit to His counsel, to trust Him wholeheartedly, to fear Him above all, and, in the end, to come to value what He values. Anything less than this is mere moralism—simply doing right because it's right, which even false religions can teach. According to the Bible, true wisdom flows out of a personal relationship with God: "The knowledge of the Holy One is understanding" (Proverbs 9:10).

Moms, teach your children how to make wise decisions, whether about marriage or other life issues. But even more importantly, encourage them to develop a personal relationship with God through Jesus, the only mediator between God and sinners (1 Timothy 2:5). Paul said that the Gospel, the message about the crucified Messiah, is "the wisdom of God" (1 Corinthians 1:24). So in pointing your children to a life of wisdom, point them to Jesus Christ.

Let the Gospel affect your parenting. —JOE

Modesty & the Heart Behind It

READ 1 TIMOTHY 2:8–15 & 1 PETER 3:1–7

"Women should adorn themselves in respectable apparel,
with modesty and self-control."

1 TIMOTHY 2:9–10

Modesty is a strange word. In normal conversation it describes humility, the opposite of pride. But in churches it usually describes a way of dressing that can be summarized as *longer* (hemlines), *higher* (necklines), and *looser* (well…*everything*). Interestingly, the Bible calls for both: modest apparel that evidences a modest attitude.

Scripture commands women to dress in modest apparel. Both 1 Timothy 2:9 and 1 Peter 3:3 deal forthrightly with an extremely practical part of everyday life for Christian women: the proper way to think about clothing, jewelry, hairstyles, and make-up. First, we should understand what the Bible is *not* saying. It does not condemn giving reasonable attention to your outward appearance. There is no particular virtue to being unattractive. Frumpiness is *not* next to godliness. God made you with a feminine beauty and a love for beauty. That's part of the image of God in you. So the passages aren't condemning beautiful clothing or hairstyles. What are they saying, then?

- You shouldn't dress (or behave) in such a way that draws overt attention to yourself, especially your sexuality. Doing so dishonors the Lord, makes you responsible for causing others to sin, communicates that you are "interested," and attracts the kind of attention that no Christian lady should want.

- You shouldn't dress intentionally backward, either. Even if you're mini-skirt-less, you may need to dump your frumpy jumpers. An overtly out-of-date wardrobe can be immodest, too, especially when worn as an advertisement of presumed virtue. The point is, don't be ostentatious in your appearance, whether through extreme frumpiness, scantiness, dressiness, casualness, or strangeness.

- You shouldn't overemphasize your outward appearance. Too many Christian women are obsessed with fashion. Not you? Consider these tests: Do you find yourself rolling your eyes or mocking the outfit of ladies with less fashion sense? Do you spend more time reading fashion magazines than Scripture? Is your love of fashion an imbalanced part of your personality in the minds of your friends? If so, you're probably overemphasizing your outward appearance. Which leads to our next point…

Scripture commands women to demonstrate a modest attitude. 1 Timothy 2:9 and 1 Peter 3:4 both move past your outward appearance to address your character, where the Gospel leaves its mark. Paul tells women to "dress up" in good works. Your godly conduct and kindness should be more noticeable than your clothes. Peter concurs, commanding you to spend some time doing your "spiritual make-up," if you will. Many ladies who would never leave their homes without primping go out day after day without taking care of their souls. Yet, soul beauty—a "gentle and quiet spirit"—is far more important and enduring than the condition of your skin, hair, or hose. In fact, Peter says that such character is what God Himself finds to be "very precious" in a lady. That should catch your attention!

The goal of godly women is to be like Christ, not some artificially-enhanced model. (Remember, even she's not that pretty!) Such Gospel-inspired modesty is irrepressibly beautiful!

Let the Gospel affect your appearance and attitude. —CHRIS

Older Women as Models & Mentors
READ TITUS 2

Older women likewise are to be reverent in behavior,
not slanderers or slaves to much wine.
They are to teach what is good, and so train the young women....

TITUS 2:3-4

Paul's basic concern in his small letter to Pastor Titus was to remind him and those under his care that belief affects behavior (2:1, 10). Paul wanted nothing to do with a mere academic knowledge of the Bible. He didn't want people to profess faith in Christ but have no life to back it up (1:16). Instead, he wanted church leaders to help Christians "connect the dots" between sound doctrine and everyday life. So in Titus 2, Paul told Titus how the truth of the Gospel should affect the lives of older men (2:2), older women (2:3), younger women (2:4-5), younger men (2:6-8), and slaves (2:9-10).

In Titus 2:3-5 Paul gives advice to two groups—older and younger women. As I approach the passage, I find myself in a pastoral dilemma: "How do I define who fits into the 'older women' category without offending anyone who may be reading this?" I'm going to play it safe and let you decide. Suffice it to say that the older women are those with experience in Christian living, marriage, parenting, and home management—those who are prepared to be mentors rather than learners.

It's noteworthy that godliness is of much higher priority to Paul than age or experience. The qualities that God prioritizes in this passage are reverence, loving speech, and self-control. *Reverence* refers to a woman who is committed to Christ in every facet of her life. *Loving speech* refers not only to the absence of sinful communication such as gossip, but also the presence of speech that is continually gracious and edifying (see Ephesians 4:29). After 25 years of pastoral experience, John Calvin put his neck on the line when he said, "Talkativeness is a disease of women, and it is increased by old age" (Calvin's commentary on Titus 2:3). Third, godly women are marked by *self-control*, freedom from excess and addiction in every part of life. What qualifies older women to pass on their wisdom, then, is godly character. They should teach both by their words and their examples.

It's also noteworthy that Paul doesn't give Pastor Titus the primary responsibility of teaching the younger women how to live out their faith in the home. Rather, he lays that burden on the older women in the church. There are several likely reasons for this. First, and most obviously, Titus wasn't an experienced wife and mom! Second, it would protect Titus from deep personal involvement in the lives of younger women, a situation which could easily set both individuals up for temptation to emotional and moral compromise. Third, it would strengthen the unity of the church to have every member involved in ministry (see Ephesians 4:1-16). So, if you are "an older woman," God calls you to be the primary mentor of younger women in your local church, whether teens or singles, young wives or mothers. And if you are "a younger woman," recognize that God has designed the church to be a place where you can find helpful counsel from godly mentors. Both younger and older women need to participate in what we often celebrate at Tri-County Bible Church as "Every Member Ministry!"

The specific lessons which Paul urges mature Christian ladies to convey to their younger sisters will be addressed very briefly tomorrow. For now, embrace this concept: Christian growth results in Christian service. Learn how the Gospel affects real life, then pass it on.

Let the Gospel affect your fellowship with other women. —JOE

School for Younger Women
READ TITUS 2

Train the young women...that the word of God may not be reviled.

TITUS 2:4-5

As we learned yesterday, I, as a young pastor, am not called to be the primary trainer of young women regarding the specifics of Christian living in the home. God has called the older women in the church to do that. I will, however, point out from Titus 2:4-5 the kinds of questions younger women should be asking and older women should be ready to answer.

1. How do I cultivate a deeper affection for my husband? The term for *love* in this passage means *affection*. It's referring to expressive adoration, rather than sacrificial action. The older women in the church should be ready to advise younger wives how to fight to keep their affections for their husbands hot.

2. How do I cultivate a deeper affection for my children? While most mothers don't struggle with serving their children, many struggle with maintaining warm affection for them in the course of day-in-day-out life (especially after sleepless nights or during days of persistent rebellion). Titus 2:4 says they should work at it with the help of godly mentors.

3. How do I pursue self-control? Older women should be experienced in the Spirit-enabled mastery of their appetites, emotions, thoughts, schedules, and priorities.

4. How do I pursue purity? In this context, the word *pure* means *sexually chaste*. Especially today when the beauty industries are multi-billion dollar businesses and where mass media pushes promiscuity as the norm, older Christian women should help their younger sisters fight for their purity (see 1 Corinthians 7:2).

5. How do I effectively manage my household? Most women are called to a seemingly impossible juggling act: raising kids, preparing meals, keeping a clean home, shopping, even teaching school or working a job, for many. Though not every woman will have the same approach, abilities, or responsibilities, older women should be able and ready to provide counsel regarding how to "juggle."

6. How do I cultivate greater kindness and generosity toward others? Amid the demands of daily life just mentioned, ministry to others can get put on the shelf. Older women should be ready to empathize with this difficulty and offer practical, biblical suggestions for young women who can't seem to keep up with their own responsibilities, let alone think about ministering to others.

7. How do I cultivate a submissive spirit toward my husband? Defining submission is fairly easy; living it out is not. Younger women should be turning to older women for help.

Older women, are you ready to give biblical, tried-and-true answers to these and other questions? Younger women, are God's concerns your concerns? And are you seeking the wise counsel of older Christian women? Are you teachable? You need to be, especially because each of these practical matters is tied to the Gospel—they are consistent with and enabled by Gospel truth (2:1), they keep the Gospel message from being reviled (2:5), they are what the saving grace of God trains us to do (2:11), and they are motivated by an anticipation of the soon return of Jesus, the one who gave Himself for us (2:13-14). It is essential that you learn from godly examples to "connect the dots" between what you believe and how you live.

Let the Gospel affect how you live out your faith at home. —JOE

Family–Like Relationships
READ 1 TIMOTHY 4:1–5:2

*Do not rebuke an older man but encourage him as you would a father,
younger men as brothers, older women as mothers,
younger women as sisters, in all purity.*

1 TIMOTHY 5:1-2

One of the areas in which Christians are most influenced by the world is in our thinking about the opposite sex. Even if we're not audaciously immoral, most men and women struggle to think properly about relationships between men and women. Some struggle with lust, thinking of the opposite sex merely as objects of pleasure (whether real or imagined). Some struggle with the desire to be lusted *after*, talking, dressing, and behaving in ways that scream, "Look at me!" Still others evaluate a person's worth based on this appearance, assuming that a person who has "the look" is deserving of attention while one who is too short, or too heavy, or simply unattractive (by the warped standards of the Hollywood elite) is unworthy of our time or thought. Whether are "attraction antennas" are up to dismiss, to notice, or to be noticed, Scripture forbids all such thinking. Instead, Paul tells us in 1 Timothy 5:1-2 to promote family-like relationships.

We should think of church members as family members. The relationships we have with fellow Christians, especially in the local church, should be precious to us. Paul tells us to think of older men and women as parents and of younger men and women as brothers and sisters. That's not rhetoric. Rather, it describes the relationships we have with each other as a result of our common adoption into the family of God (1 John 3:1; 4:7-8, 21). Indeed, many Christians find that their relationships with fellow Christians are deeper and more encouraging than those with their natural families.

We should respect and encourage each other. Paul tells Timothy not to rebuke an older Christian, but to encourage him. The same counsel holds for younger Christians, as well. Treating each other like family doesn't mean that we are free to blast each other. It requires affection and honor. It also requires family-like transparency as we graciously push each other toward godliness.

Finally, we should promote purity with each other. There is one person in the world with whom you should be flirtatious and intimate, and that's your husband. Other men and women—whether they are attractive or not—should be the objects of your Christian affection, but not of your sensual attentions. It is no more acceptable to lust after a sibling in Christ than to lust after a natural-born brother or sister. Nor may you encourage such lust in others. To be blunt, it's as perverse to tempt a man in the church as to seduce your own father or brother. We need to put our "attraction antennas" down.

Healthy families love each other unconditionally. They help each other. They respect each other. They don't use each other. They don't judge each other on the basis of appearance. They protect each other from temptation and danger. They promote each other's growth. That's how we should relate to each other in the church—with family-like relationships.

Let the Gospel affect your relationships in the church. —CHRIS

Luke, "the Gospel for Women"
READ LUKE 1:1–56

And the twelve were with him, and also some women.

LUKE 8:1-3

Alfred Plummer wrote that Luke is "in an especial sense the Gospel for women. Jew and Gentile alike looked down on women. But all through this Gospel they are allowed a prominent place" (*The Gospel According to S. Luke*, xlii). Luke frequently records episodes that involve women, including accounts that are not recorded in any of the other Gospel records. Each of these records highlights the love that God has for women. I've listed several of them below with a brief explanation and thought for personal application.

1. Elizabeth and Mary: Lovers of God's Word (ch. 1-2). Elizabeth and her husband, Zechariah, were exemplary in their obedience to the Old Testament (1:6). And from Mary's poetic reaction to the angel's message, it's clear that she knew the Old Testament well (1:46-55). She quotes from 1 Samuel 2:1-10 and Psalms 103 and 107. A primary mark of a godly woman is treasuring the Bible and trusting the God it reveals.

2. Anna: A Prayer Warrior (2:36-38). After seven years of marriage, Anna's husband died. For the rest of her life (probably more than 50 years) she faithfully served the Lord as a "widow prayer warrior." Don't underestimate the power of a widow's prayers! (See also the parable in Luke 18:1-8.)

3. Two Women: Recipients of Jesus' Compassion. Jesus had compassion on a widow's grief (7:11-15) and healed a woman who had long-term physical and spiritual problems (13:10-17). Don't think that Jesus is unconcerned about your sicknesses, trials, and weaknesses.

4. A Repentant Prostitute: A Trophy of Grace (7:36-50). "A woman in the city who was a sinner" interrupted a meal to worshipfully anoint Jesus' feet. Jesus assured her that she was forgiven, praised her expression of love, and convicted self-righteous Simon with her example. He delights in the worship of disreputable sinners who have repented.

5. Many Women: Financial Supporters (8:1-3). Luke names three women who both followed and funded Jesus and His disciples. He says that there were many others as well. It's clear that several of these women had notorious backgrounds. God will never forget the worship of women that give their time and money to the cause of Christ. (See also the brief account in Luke 21:1-4.)

6. Mary: A Devoted Listener (10:38-42). In choosing to "listen to the Lord's teaching" Mary chose what was best, even as her sister wearied herself with service. Beware of being too busy to have time with Jesus! Time spent at the feet of Jesus is an investment you'll never regret.

7. Weeping Women: Reflections of Jesus' Heart (23:27-30). With great sympathy and grief, many women followed the suffering Savior on the road to Golgotha. In a stunning display of selflessness, Jesus revealed again His heart for His people (as in 19:41-44). He urged the women not to lament Him, but their own generation and future generations who would experience the outpouring of God's wrath because of their continued rejection of Him. Christ-like women should sorrow for the unrepentant world around them.

The examples and ministries of godly women were invaluable in Jesus' day. They remain invaluable today.

Let the Gospel embolden you for ministry. —JOE

"Neither Do I Condemn You"

READ JOHN 8:1–11 & ROMANS 8:1, 34

Neither do I condemn you; go, and from now on sin no more.

JOHN 8:11

People are fond of saying "there are two kinds of people in the world." With an eye on the first part of John 8, I offer this generality: "There are two kinds of people in the world—those who are scandalized by their own sins, and those who are scandalized by the sins of others." The *condemners* are dominated by proud self-righteousness, a sin more grievous than whatever they are shocked by in others. The *condemned* are candidates for God's grace.

The story recorded in John 8:1-11 begins with Jesus teaching crowds in the Temple (8:1-2). The scribes and Pharisees, the "condemners" of their day, were jealous of Christ's influence, and they brought before Him a notorious sinner. Christ was the one in their crosshairs, of course, but they were all too willing to sacrifice an ashamed woman in order to entrap Him. The woman's nakedness was probably barely covered, perhaps with a sheet hastily wrapped around her, for she had been "caught in the act of adultery" (8:4). She probably kept her eyes downward, knowing that she was justly condemned by her accusers, including herself. The men, on the other hand, piously said that Moses' Law called for her to be stoned, then asked Christ for His recommendation. They were ready to pounce upon her—and Him (8:6).

Jesus' response was astonishing. Rather than speaking, He began writing on the ground, perhaps writing a summary of the 10 commandments to remind the crowd that there were nine more in addition to the one of which the woman was accused. When the accusers pressed Christ for an answer, He confronted them with their own sin: "Let him who is without sin among you be the first to throw a stone at her" (8:7). Ashamed, they quietly dispersed, leaving Christ alone with the guilty woman (8:8-9). Jesus brought to her attention the fact that none had condemned her (8:10), then said something more amazing still: "Neither do I condemn you; go, and from now on sin no more." (8:11).

What a striking contrast! Men who were guilty of sin themselves and therefore had no right to condemn anyone were still eager to do so. What hypocrisy! And the sinless Savior, the only person in history who did have the right to condemn her, declined to do so. What mercy! Why did Jesus not pick up stones to cast at her and them, since He was "without sin"? Because His God-given mission at His first advent was not to condemn the world, but to save it (John 3:17). That's the very point of Romans 8:34. The one entrusted by God the Father to condemn sinners (which He will do at His second coming) is Jesus—the very one who died and rose again to save those who repent of their sins and trust Him as Savior. He does not condemn sinners because He would condemned *for* sinners at Calvary. There is, then, no condemnation for those who are in Christ Jesus (Romans 8:1)!

We live in a sin-cursed world. All of us fail miserably and repeatedly. With that in mind, in humility, be more aware of your own sins than the sins of others. And in faith, be more aware of Christ's pardoning death than of either.

That's as good a place as any to wrap up our month-long study of Gospel living. By grace, you can be a pardoned and changed sinner rather than a self-righteous condemner of others—or yourself. Run to Christ, the only hope for sinners like us.

Let the Gospel give you hope. —CHRIS